By Gary Beck

Novels

Extreme Change
Acts of Defiance
Flawed Connections
Call to Valor
Sudden Conflicts
Crumbling Ramparts

Flare UP
Raise High the Walls
Still Defiant
State of Rage
Wave Length
Protective Agency
Obsess

Poetry

Expectations
Days of Destruction
Dawn in Cities
Assault on Nature
Songs of a Clerk
Civilized Ways
Conditioned Response
Displays
Perceptions
Fault Lines
Tremors
Virtual Living
Perturbations
Blossoms of Decay
Rude Awakenings
Blunt Force

Remission of Orde
Contusions
Transitions
Earth Links
Mortal Coil
Desperate Seeker
Too Harsh For Pastels
Temporal Dreams
Severance
Redemption Value
Fractional Disorder
Disruptions
Ignition Point
Learning Curve
Resonance

Play Collections
The Big Match and other one act plays
Collected Plays of Gary Beck Volume I
Plays of Aristophanes translated then directed by Gary Beck
Collected Plays of Gary Beck Volume II

Short Story Collections
A Glimpse of Youth
Now I Accuse and other stories
Dogs Don't Send Flowers and other stories

Essays
Collected Essays of Gary Beck

Resonance

Gary Beck

Oui puisque je retrouve un ami si fidele, ma fortune va prendre un face nouvelle.

- Racine

I found myself more concerned with the message, rather than the 'poetic' quality of poetry. I saw the arts begin to turn progressively inward, not in the nature of profound meditation, or seeking deeper understanding, but more in the aspect of flaunting personal agonies and confessions. This is what our culture has wrought. It satiates the consciousness with an endless stream of pictorial imagery that stupefies the visual sense and degrades the uniqueness of verbal description. So poets, increasingly shunted aside by a growing public preference for non-stop tv, turned to baring their guts in anguished revelations of childhood abuse, or indignation for their neglected feelings. This type of indulgence and I are incompatible. To me, poetry is greater than my personal sufferings. I feel there should be room in the chambers of poetry for alternatives to academic products and disclosures of angst. I have chosen my own direction and have evolved to expressing thoughts and feelings about issues. And if I may have abandoned metaphor and simile, it is not that I despise them, but I must deliver what I believe to be a necessary blunt message. In an age of increasing insecurity and danger, we must still cherish poetry. But the guardians of the gates of poetry should allow examination of the problems of the world, with direct communication, in order to extend the diminishing influence of poetry on the events of our times.

An excerpt from Gary Beck's essay 'The Evolution of Poetry', published by The Recusant

Poems from 'Resonance' have appeared in:

Aberration Labyrinth, Camroc Press Review, Catapult to Mars, Clutching At Straws, Counterexample Poetics, Dead Snakes, Diverse Voices Quarterly, East Coast Literary Review, Edwin E. Smith's Quarterly Magazine, ExPat Lit, Glassworks Magazine, Hitherto MUIC Literary Journal, Indigo Rising, Infinite Press: A Literary Journal, Inwood Indiana Press (Prolific Press), Madswirl, MediaVirus Magazine, Oberon's Law, Philly Flash Inferno, Poem2Day, Prairie Wolf Press Review, Protest Poems, Quantum Poetry Magazine, Red Ochre Press, Rivets Litmag, Sassafras Literary Magazine, Spudgun Magazine (CCC Press), Stepping Stones Magazine:Almia (FS Press), Strange Road, Structo Magazine, The Adroit Journal, The Plebian Rag, The Rainbow Rose Ezine, The Rusty Truck, The Scrambler, The Shine Journal, The Write Place at the Right Time, Vanilla Literary & Art Journal (Vanilla Press), Vapid Kitten, Vis a Tergo, Vox Poetica, West Ward Quarterly, Symmetry Pebbles, Pyrta, Bluestem Magazine, Skive Press & Westview.

Some poems from Resonance appeared in a chapbook, Electronic Loss and other poems published by Fowlpox Press.

Contents

Dire Prediction

Service men and women,
firefighters,
police officers,
military,
other functionaries
vital to society
insufficiently appreciated
by bloated consumers
frequently sheltered
from traumas of life.
Now that we are removing
the capable blue-collar class,
outsourcing jobs abroad
complementing the flight of capital,
the growth of servitude jobs
does not inspire confidence
that we will retain
men and women
who will walk through fire, bullets, blood,
to protect us.

Street Lore

When I was young
insufficiently educated boys
demonstrated scholarship
learning dirty words
in foreign languages.
On today's harsher streets
linguistic ability
has been replaced
by slang and curses,
almost unintelligible
to evolved citizens.

Children of Deprivation

In the world of power,
men stand by the buttons
of weapons of mass destruction,
eager to slay millions,
while we sit in comfort in our homes
newspapered, tv'd, dreamy,
careless of our sentinels, foes.
And our hungry children,
hollow from the cornucopia of science
know swollen barns of grain
rotting on a distant government preserve
will never be theirs, despite their need.
So trapped in tenements, shanties
they hate their mothers, siblings,
always poised to detonate.

Possession

It is after midnight.
I lie alone
contorted on my bed,
room lined with
books, pictures, records,
a dozen poems on my desk,
works of beauty wisdom joy wild hearty lusty
obscene reverent ecstatic maudlin curious
erotic mad exuberance and find
imprisoned by my depth of learning feeling searching,
the memory of your too brief possession
paints your face upon a plaster-peeling ceiling,
splays your thighs across a molting rug
preens your breasts upon a eunuch bed,
amiable and insolent.
The arabs in my kitchen
rest their arms on six foot muskets,
chew beetle,
talk of ancient caravans,
maidens.
God is great.
Examining the invisible evidence of my desire
I smoke a final cigarette.
disdain a blindfold and say:
"I can't forget you."

Radiation Rhapsody

Strum a chord for me,
and I shall improvise....

Sparrows sit upon window-sills
watching in bewilderment
as snot-nosed children
cower under desks
in schoolrooms of the world,
while daddy's working hard,
building rockets....

Presidents and Premiers
(protocol is not forgotten)
send each other formal notes,
while people read pamphlets
of nuclear survival.

Shall I be a garbage man
and haul away the ashes?
But who will haul away my ashes,
if the whole world crashes?

Ride with me....
Put your farecard in the turnstile to annihilation.
The "A" train stops at Times Square station,
opens pneumatic doors,
ejects crowds whose rhinoceros roars
are silenced by a blinding flash,
a sudden flood of molten slag.

No more rush hour.
No quick latté at Starbucks.
Just a large crater
that will glow at night
for the next hundred years.

Dreams of Home

Exiles remember lands of plenty
fragmenting themselves
into disembodied continuations
spinning through cycles of endurance
that have little resemblance
to the fountains of compassion
that exiles always crave,
until gradual disappearance,
their fading no cataclysm,
but narcotic languor
too wearied for splendors,
eroded beyond compelling,
wanting moments of resurrection
before unfervent destruction.

The Song of Squalor

Now in the silence of evening
there is a plaintive chant
of many mourners calling
for resurrection of the senses.
Hear voices of sorrow
raised to gods of yesteryear,
crying, lamenting
for the solitary death
of former hopes.
Out of the failing heart of man
with alms of consolation
comes quietly
the spirit of love,
to prevail evermore.
Sing. Sing. In many tongues,
a thousand ended dreams
forgotten, then remembered
in the chastity of peace.

Opium Escape

I watched you walk away
out of my dark, bewildered life.
I cursed you, then.

I drove home alone remembering
how many nights spent with no one else to interfere
with some strange communion passing between us
as we devoured each other like sacred wafers
having nothing but hollow reed jutting up
to suck when we gasped for lack of air.

Never again
is a long, long time.
I knew that you would never call.
I stripped, alone,
looking in the mirror
at my severed body,
raw and ulcered in the places
where your body merged.

I remembered
how many arguments when writhing in some hostile land
we looked upon each other and found a stranger's face
staring in tedium, indifference, loathing,
until trying to build too much too fast and failing,
cried that you were not what you seemed to be
and never, never, NEVER would be.

Sleep beckoned like a hungry cannibal.
Dreamless, I crawled into escape from you,
pulled the zipper closed behind me,
snuggled to my pillow,
took one last puff on my opium pipe,
found you and….

Before They Turn to Dust

Old men wake the restless hands of war
and imagine sabers in paneled rooms.
They are the makers of power
who have forgotten their speeches
made to men and women
who carried bayonets to other lands,
promising a lasting peace.
When lights burn late in domed buildings
they are spending our children
and while we sleep,
a ghost paces the beaches of Elba,
watching the sky for omens.
Siren Song

Singing daggers,
unctuous voices croon
promising advancements.
The foolish are impaled on barbs,
the fearful sit and hope,
the hardy risk the game
and win and lose.

Singing daggers,
tempting hands beckon
signaling kindness.
The weak drop by the wayside,
cowards run for safety,
the daring risk all
and fail or conquer.

Beware the song,
hands concealing daggers,
smiles not assurance,
just daily tunes of betrayal
treating promises
like neglected orphans,
abandoned to coincidence.

Convert

Lost in silence
my soul howls
and finds no comfort.
As bold as Vikings
I set out to gorge
on plundered lands
misplaced in streams of patience.
I sing no expectations,
my crumbling moments of desire
will not stir the deafened world
that I'll woo now
with bombs and arson.

Continuations

People don't like certain questions,
especially why we are here.
That's why fathers give sons
a name with a number after it,
call them junior,
to compel a link to the past.
Is this benefit or betrayal?
Thinking dilutes the breed
that considers the present,
neglecting the future.
Myopics of tomorrow
hope that short sight
is improbably balanced
by acts of charity.

This is the voice of one man singing... About the Cuban Missile Crisis – October, 1962

Boy, dey yanked me outa the warmtha
me mudders body.
Wow, dey beat me when I played
wit meself.
Dey made me go to school
and listen to all da crap.
My old man kicked my ass
when I played hookey.
I went to high school,
joined a gang.
I got caught stealin.
The cops beat me up.
I quit school
knocked up a broad
and her old man made me marry her.
We got two fuggin kids
who never stop screamin.
The fuggin house is fallin ta pieces.
The fuggin union wants more dues.
The snotty bastard at the bowling alley
always makes these wise cracks.
The fuggin phone company
is shuttin off the phone.
The old lady is a fuggin slob.
After a hard day's work
I can't even sit down and enjoy a fuggin can of beer.
I hope they use their fuggin rockets.

Recollections

I followed the blind course of my desire
hungering some undiscovered future,
lusting for poetry, great feasts, beautiful women.
At first all things fell short of expectations,
but there was enough joy to make my song.
Yet sometimes as I wandered the web of hunger,
an unforgotten face peered from the dark curtain
and reminded me of ancient ambitions…. Failures.
I searched for words of greeting, wanting to say:
"You are my memories, the only wealth I own."
Instead I asked: "How have you been?
What are you doing now?"
My mind a drab Seigneur, bereft of power,
uttering no protestations
as the resurrected ghost, remembrance,
despoils my last domain, the bitter past.

Old Age

Between the moment of decline,
the last splurge
peering in the mirror of power,
erasing hopes of tribute
from Caesar's conquests,
youth's unebbing hunger
is eternal and denied.
Images in the glass
provoke unhidden derision
sparkling with kindless delight
at failure as drab as age,
posturing a weak reflection,
lasting as long as joy.

Haunted

Time passes to the count
of a threatened pulse,
as we sit silently
an imagined ghost.
Atoms of despair clash
in seething arteries,
as the veins of thought throb,
incessant as a midnight drum
thumping a hidden message
in the night.
Ravished by finding
our own fear,
captured by the serpent-spell
of paranoid confession sins,
we sit within our body's walls
seeking an asylum of stillness
to tranquilize restless limbs.

The Poet

Too often have I turned
to others in supplication,
crying my need like wares.
I waited with expectations,
thinking words of promise true,
undone by my desires.
I am tired of patience
weary of bland refusals.
I shall never soar through others
and remain within my room
making poems to hide my fears,
dreaming bombs to crush deniers.

Fond Pause

The drifting instant of an afternoon
sun-touching your smile's memory,
thoughts of musty windmills,
mouse ghosts
unsqueeking in shuddering rafters,
the creak and groan of departure,
your hunger for the day.

Dwindling to small eruptions
beyond compelling us
fugitive to tranquility,
spewing our mouthings of tomorrow,
most sacred spirit, tomorrow.

Weary of enchantment
other permutations
flex the impossible,
stretch and roll it finger near
until beyond imagining,
curling gently into silence,
sit, sigh, be still.

Done dreaming,
you are denied comfort,
visions exhausted,
packed in a postal crate
that may or may not arrive.

Sad Mate

Your carnal fingers
that have me adored,
ran sensual spectacles
that left me bored.
My flesh unlit
by any passionate device,
absorbed hands, mouth, womb,
implacable as ice.
O woman thrashing
from your pleasure overpowering,
I lie empty and remote,
you lie sated and devouring.

Fanciful Dream

Mighty empires could not endure
my life's perpetual burning,
impaled on tortuous spit,
roasts my bones char burnt,
innards beyond resurrection,
taunting me to rise again,
preparing for surprise again,
braise, season, stir, steam
by mad chef in lunatic dream,
oils and mixes to perfection
horrible chambers of delight,
seating legally, two hundred,
small house, small gate,
enough circumspect viewers
delicately observing vital operation,
masked, gowned, shoed and gloved,
upper atmosphere snowflake clean,
nothing dainty, just substantial
moments of serious intention
leading to oblivious condition.
Cut, parry, lunge, disengage,
it's not supposed to be a stage.
Strip, shower, dry, dress, sleep,
good grief, there should be more….
Keep trying. Ask…. And it shall be….

Rant

Death to tyrants,
man the barricades,
come my people
long oppressed and pillaged,
turn labor's hands to weapons.
Let the eaters of your flesh
hear your wrath and tremble.
You are mighty, good people,
so seize what is yours by right
and let the....
Wow, look at those legs....
Why am I standing here ranting?
Hey, baby....

Find the Path

I do not sing that dreaming
makes the poet free,
for he must touch life
like other men
and when young,
nourished on opulent books,
nurtured on frustration,
how easy to escape to castles
with spires of fancy.
When the crabby monitor
handles the singer
with ungentle pincers,
waking him
to the twisted ways of man,
look hard, tormented one
and choose your song,
or seek another place
in this contrived world.

Two Songs of Lust

Blondly erotic
with lost eyes
she chokes from too much wanting.
I feel some pity,
but mostly
would lay hands
upon her body.

She walks by,
a triangle between her thighs
cripples her.
She is soft,
like fingers holding rotten plums,
hips an agonized rotation
summoning hands
to roam her body
that I cannot resist.

Zoo Threat

The leopard prowls from wall to wall
cursing the bars with flame eyes,
climbs like housecat to its perch,
yawns elegantly,
full of dangerous grace,
stretches black-spot length,
sits,
watches the watchers,
speaks with jungle tongue:
Sssssss
I will get loose.
Sssssss
I will find your children in their lair.
Sssssss
I will pet them with my claws for throwing peanuts.
I will kiss them with my fangs for laughing.
I can wait.
One dark night…. I'll be free.

Idle Conceits

On the journey to the sea
the years have brought
the endless, timeless,
roar of ocean
whose spermy, frothy waves
break upon the shore
in rolling, crashing currents
that fall and leave
green-yellow maiden-hair
upon the beach
uncombed.
Then, blowing a final wind
on Assyrian sands
Nature crawls into a steamer trunk
and goes to Bermuda
for the mild winter.

City Exhudation

It is the silent hour of evening.
Rain falls in blackening drops,
the coat of daytime slime creeps into sewers
that carry off the remains of man.
Night-walkers possess the waste,
lonely footsteps echo in the gloom,
as city vapors curate the streets
and cloak the lost in darkness.

Separation

I ache with unending sorrow
for the love I lost,
and still the squirrel leaps
happily from limb to limb
in his comforting tree,
and the little children
play on the see-saw,
and the pigeons hop and flutter,
intent on saving their lives
from desperate homicides on bicycles
riding the last enactment.

Chance Encounter

In the strangeness of our meeting
eyes lambent, flaming insects
flickering in the night of parting,
loss passed from self to self.
You are undiscovered
a continent met for exploring.
As fearful as a castaway
inured to the isle of despair,
I dream illusory glimpses
of the ship of rescue.

Severance

Let us talk no more of patient dreams,
our lives have turned to madness.
Relentless as a tartar horde
we sack the village of our souls.
Together we fire the drowsing world
and in incendiary shadows
turn, strip each other bare,
fall upon each other's flesh,
roll until we die in cinders,
then wipe the dripping remnants
on a torn and grimy towel,
face each other from afar,
remote as distant stars
that witness fading love,
light two cigarettes
and dream alone.

Electronic Loss

I lost my love in a telephone booth
in a drugstore on Broadway.
It cost twenty five cents.

I lost my precious gifts of time,
joy,
her teeth fastened to my neck.

I heard her voice
remote,
speaking in another tongue
I could not understand.

I screamed in anguish,
love,
need,
I want to nibble on your ear lobe.

She could not hear me.
A rancorous operator translated:
"I'll call you if I change my mind".

I stood at the counter,
paid for an aspirin heart
and went home
to listen for the telephone.

Sequoias

I walk a lonely path past dying trees,
their limbs outstretched in supplicating pleas.
Their tale of woe I do not know
of desolate years alone.
They stalwartly stand, in vigilance grand,
embracing the wind with a groan.
The path unfolds, in awe I catch my breath,
all splendor gone in such majestic death.
Their prime has passed, I view the last
impressive monarchs made
and now I attend their tragical end
and watch nature's handiwork fade.

Indulgence

The old caretaker
of creeping time,
intent on deceiving people,
sometimes disguises himself
and wears a little bonnet
with little wings upon it.
The way to trick a caretaker
intent on depriving people,
is to trap him in a moment's lapse
and spin the wheel of time
without his supervision.

Poet's Fantasy

I leave a million things unsaid
before I grow another tongue
to curse the poet's failure.
How easy to be careless,
neglect the craft of verse
when lusting to sing words of power
that strike the reader like a knife thrust,
puncturing the soul with visions.

Twisted Love

My love is like a ravaged rose
that lost petals in copulation.
She calls me daddy,
wants me to protect her,
but plays with herself
when she thinks I'm sleeping.
I only knew her three days
and she called me her wild lover.
Soon she will go to another,
too demented to be constant.

Respite

The stranger comes along the way,
sees the children carelessly at play,
watches with sad and lonely smile,
emerges from his thoughts a tender while.
The stranger goes along the way,
past the children carelessly at play,
no longer watching with that smile,
sad, lonely, but tender, for a while.

Revery

Frequently my thoughts begin to stray
to wild, green woods
where happy children play
and in the innocent serenity
sorrow is apart from me.
For in the smell of liberty
that lies in lonely paths
I see glimmers of futurity
that comes from loving life,
apart from human strife.

Departed

In a dream of another land,
in the warmth of another room,
my beloved lies in her bed,
with someone else at her side.
I sit alone in the night,
burning for her in the night,
aching with pain for my love,
lost without hope of return.

Fatal Wound

Another night has passed,
witness to our perjured love.
I listen to the footsteps
coming up the stairs
that go past my door.
It is not you.
I go back to the window
and watch the street of life.
The footsteps that pass me by
are more terrible than daggers
thrusting into soft flesh.
They shatter the unspoken hope
of love's salvation.

Rebel's Plaint

A death knell sounds orchestrally,
bodies shudder,
arm-pits leak,
fingers twitch.
Curse the generals of the world,
the senators and party secretaries,
the rocket building,
rocket aiming,
workers against the world,
united for our inevitable destruction,
and scream to anyone who listens,
about sunsets,
lying with your girl friend on a beach
in pre-global warming summer,
watching the fog roll in from the Pacific,
walking through a snowstorm in Nebraska,
listening to robins singing of spring.
We have listened to the lies in silence
that lead us to devolution.
We have read about the politics, passively
that bring endless armaments construction.
We should heal the world of raging madness,
before we are doomed forever
to an obliterating madhouse.

Mythos

Tonight the wind
goes howling and shrieking
through naked trees,
making them groan
in unnatural agony.
The creaking of frigid limbs
splits the darkness
as the wild hunt goes on.
Every moaning shrub and plant,
each sob of nature,
save for the ugly one
who cackles in her cursed den,
reaches Asgard with lamentations,
for there, transfixed,
lies Balder, dead.

Death of a Stranger

A body fell on a city sidewalk.
A thousand brothers saw it die.
They watched in incredulous awe
in the shadows of gravestone buildings
and feasted their eyes
while maggots crept the streets,
until they walked away,
unmournful.

Rejected Citizens

Through the midnight darkness
of indifferent cities,
despairing dwellers
pass their lives
in one-night, cheap hotels,
walk lonely streets,
pausing for brief moments
to talk to human fixtures
attached to street lamps,
then pass on.

Query

Down the fiery streets of time
at burning noon and ash midnight,
I pass the city faces bleak
that stare with vacant eyes.
Each searing glance a question asks:
who stole our liberty?
I have no answer
that will satisfy.

.

Bleak Highway

It is inky night.
We are driving, driving, driving
into the impenetrable blackness
of the heart of America.
There are no stars visible,
just never-ending darkness
broken only
by the passing gleam of headlights
from wanderers forever lost
in a confusing land.

Shattered Dream

And the people went out of their houses
and stood together in the night,
and a great star flickered in the night,
and a great light covered the land,
and peace was born.
And men no longer went into the night
to slay their neighbors,
women no longer sat in the cold night
barren,
children no longer went hungry.
Then the night passed
the day burned bright
and people awakened to sorrow.

Dim Illusion

In many men
the little part, still boy
keeps fading illusions,
that once,
loved and cherished
by a father's strength,
a mother's soft caress,
they retreated to a citadel
to tend their wounds.

This place of roots

though puny refuge,
yet haven in despair,
held puissant awe,
until demanded.
Then shutting out the seeker,
like temple doors
barred to the defiler,
that song of need
wove unreal myths,
remembered as the past.

Maureen

Huddling in the schoolyard shadows,
blond Maureen,
 overwhelmed by avalanches
of voracious spiders,
running hairy feelers
on her lonely thighs,
whimpers for a date
to take her to the Prom.

Condition Grave

What is the hunger of water-falls,
little men of tiny boats, flirting with whirlpools?
They lie upon dirty, crowded beaches,
dreaming of two weeks in July,
safaried in cameras, they tread San Juan hotels,
Miami hotels, Canadian motels.
What is the power of Sequoia trees,
tiny men of roads, chug in cars
around, between, through ancient fibers,
 storm defying, victims of axes?
The travelers sleep late, swim, press on.
This aging land, veined with highways,
bulging with cities of muscle,
boned by small towns,
arteries roads, roads, roads,
coursing its people as blood,
tainted and diseased
through a febrile body.

Trapped in Flesh

Burying myself
in your eager carnality
I lose hope of visions,
pride to dream.
Books, tears, regressions,
are crutches to my frayed soul
that must escape the torment
of your devouring lust.

Vision Denied

If I hate myself no more,
spurn the whip,
scorn the curse
and look at myself,
the tired, lonely, frightened me
and say:
"How long my own worst foe,
blind, full of torment?"
The friendless, solitary me
knows
that bound by ignorance, pride,
most of all my hungry youth,
I fail to see
wisdom in others,
hope of peace.

Poetry

Poet's words
crouch in tall grass,
fearful rabbits hiding.
I sniff,
bide patiently,
storm explosions,
grasp,
yet elusive
they hide again.

Epic

We crippled sons
do not have our forefather's crusades
whine the ancient songs of restless men,
nasal in heated rooms.
We cry for causes, having lost
cruel hunger of other ages,
curse the test-tube plans
that guide us to new motions.
We would be led,
spearmen in Agamemnon's band.
Yes, we would despoil a city,
we office mites, subway bards,
fanciers of fair captives, distant glory,
but only the poet's song
conceals dull and gore long past.

Creator

Puzzle this creation.
Things merge,
birthing more.
Clamorings rise,
breeding change.
Things come together,
separate,
leaving parts
on a weak earth,
listless and sedate,
(an old prim ma'am
eyeing a child's soiled fingers.).

Frail Seeker

I will never speak a thousand tongues
and never see all places.
I will miss too many books and women
and the mystery of distant stars.
I am made of endless yearnings
for triumphs, skills and countless lore,
remain a stranger to serenity,
wondering my hungers.

Voyage

Far have I come
on a journey by sea
through the timeless roar of ocean,
whose spermy, broken waves
fall upon the shore
in rolling, crashing breakers
that cover virginal sand
with green-yellow maiden-hair,
uncombed, as I lie spent,
beyond evolution.

Victim

The no-sleep nights,
blossoms of recrimination,
pass with empty fury.
Idle as a pagan lord
without barbaric splendor,
I see myself as fleeting midnights
trapped in woman's eyes.

Distant Menace

Pride is the crutch
that causes our failures,
for we are old wars
waiting to happen,
while a ghost stands
on the beach of Elba
yearning for astrological configurations.
Tremors emanate outward,
people feel vibrations,
see birds of no song
ominous black wings,
sense approaching danger.

Girl Child (To Carol)

You were young
and you were fair,
and wore a speckled spider
in your hair.
You did not fear
dirty knees, soiled hands,
a true companion,
despite parental admonitions.

Consumable

He who lives in disunity
crying,
shall not be free again,
will look upon
regiments of hot eyes
casting like fishermen,
eager to take him home
to cook him for their mothers.

Baseball

Love,
da season's come.
(Ya hear me hon?)
The season's come.
Time to oil the old mitt,
stretch the arm
and think about the girls
who watch me play.

General Abuse

Ten thousand bloody bodies
lifeless on a plain,
countless thousands wounded
torn and racked by pain
creep through the empty victor
haunted by the stain
made by young men's bodies,
by his order, slain.
This man sought world power.
Ruling men seemed
the prize meant for the strongest,
where is it now, his dream?
For in the still of evening,
beneath sun-lit skies
ten thousand bloody bodies
march before his eyes,
reminding him of anguish
brought to those who weep
for those who once were living
and now forever sleep.

Art Calls

The blind years, groping my way out of school, staggering through jobs, cities, people, countries, searching for an answer, some rest from insane, driving need. Then the first seeds torn from a greedy, devouring city. Yes. Get a job, make money, acquire responsibilities. All will teach me how to apply myself to poetry. How the taste of money awakened fantasies of my teens, the hunger for possession raging through me a fatal, consuming poison. I killed me, an unborn me, a dreamy, hopeful me, as dead and pathetic as an unprotected baby.

Years of my lost time, where are you? Do you run smiling down a city street, a long-haired girl tightly welded to my hand, running with me? A purple Hudson River sunset, making a king's chamber of my shabby West Side room. The momentary tranquil peace of a lonely midnight walk. And while I brood, the city sleeps a million panther dreams, creeping in dangerous shadows around our beds.

Confined

Dripping water wears a groove
in a rough stone floor
and sunlight falls diaphanous
through black bars of containment
that will allow no escape
from a shackle bed
for the prisoner of twisted love.

Change

I think about an acquaintance,
now dead.
I never liked him,
but when I helped carry his coffin
others decided he was my friend.
In my solitude,
as cranky as a virgin spinster
brushing past the cobwebs of an attic,
then sadly turning pages of a musty album,
I look at pictures of the dead
and barely remember their faces.

Estranged

Not alone by wanting you,
or in a moment's soft caress
will you know me.
For in the troubled passing of the night
I cry louder than a thousand homeless children,
lost to heaven's delights.
I touch you often,
though you never hear my fingers whisper
that I need more than your reluctant flesh
in this world of unfulfillment.

Woeful Vision

No longer young,
but not older than me,
she is my bad dream.
I see her in the subway,
a slattern with a shopping bag
and a wrinkled face
that has forgotten smiles.

Expectant Lover

Although still a stranger,
I have awaited you
with hunger and impatience,
pacing your arrival.
I searched the walls
with constructive eyes
seeing frescos of your face,
while my fingers danced
new paths on your body.
The time-worn traveler,
slayer of my passions,
whose ominous thoughts
create fearful imaginings
that whisper protection
breeds sick misgivings,
but too lonely for concealment,
I sabotage restraint
and want you a madness.

Comfort

A little moment of dream
whispers nourishing words
in the wilderness of silence
and carries more encouragement
than transitory choruses
of imagined angels,
concert virtuosi.

This Fleeting Life

In the darkness
a stealthy mouse creeps across the creaking floor,
softly squeaking to the sagging boards
that rot and fall.
In the darkness by the window
a lonely figure sits,
silent and full of dreams.
He looks with eyes hungrier than tombs
upon the passing strangers,
passing in the darkness,
young and full of dreams.
Boards rot and fall.
A mouse feeds and squeaks his joy.
An old man slumps
upon an ancient, broken chair
and sleeps.

Sing Sorrow

If the world is cruel and strange
never sing,
for song is a carnal sorrow,
not soft as woman,
goddess of midnight visions
who tears the last song
from a battered heart.

Growth Term

The last sleep
of armless brothers
who dream no world of lovers,
nor sing the serpent,
nor ride the waterfall of time,
wakes the dark poet,
arms grown from royal palms,
careless as some god of myth
strewing fruit to winds.

O, Man. What a Night

Shall we love in pastel colorations,
a blazing sunset joining the dark sea?
Shall we twine in melodic motion,
a mad piano gentled by a violin?
Or shall we tremble in midnight whispers,
a first kiss hesitant upon a timid hand?
Oh, hell,
let's just be ourselves.
You'll whine all night
and I'll pace,
sullen and disgusted.
But then,
some word, some look,
some loving touch
and we'll fall on each other
like released prisoners
and eat each other up.
Then we go to bed.
I put you in my neck
under the big daddy covers,
we burrow together like puppies
and sleep.

Poet Agonistes

Often months of silence,
then a poem surfaces,
a cataract aroar
foaming and churning
in maniacal frenzy
carrying the great flow
of long pent words.
The nights have passed,
too many,
while I picked mangos, dates, figs,
crying some primeval curse
on my drooping stallion head.
In solitude I should choose
to have the world of madness
pass me by,
but I am trapped by destiny
and dream a better world.

Renunciation

With a passion that burns free,
in a love that will not die,
my heart embraces the sea,
my mind discovers the sky.
Will power lost in yearning,
for a woman's heart grown cold,
made me forget all learning,
as stale dreams quickly grew old.
The fire that breeds in the night
has spread despite calming sleep,
and will perish in my sight,
with the hopes I cannot keep.

Seduction

The secret longing
of your calling mouth
pushing your moist tongue
into my flesh
as my hand rides
the swelling crest
of your buttocks,
rolling the curves
with urgent fingers,
gripping pliant thighs,
as your hot flesh
urges me
to pierce your loins.

Overview

I have passed into
the non-return of fantasy,
above, the snow-shed tufts billow
in the strange air waves
that neither roll nor flow.
Below, feet of men tread earth,
mighty mountains dwarf them,
while wings of iron
 ravish God's pure realm.
Yes, to heaven, Dante cried.
Fewer men think now
they come closer
to untouched coves
where sweet souls sleep.

One Summer

The sounds of summer,
the little legs
running field to field
that fall, roll,
dirty knees smiling.
O evening,
clouds like tarnished nickels
smoking home to bed,
the last bugle from a nearby camp,
voices whispering,
kiss, parting…. Promise.
The night falls a sudden ballerina
landing in grace
on love's wet earth.

Advice

There is hope of ease
from life's gift of pain,
if we aspire to the sacred,
control the profane.

Requiescat In Pacem

That friend I had
I lost to death
who never pausing to explain
moved on.
And the fervor that gave him breath
empowered the young hunger
dreaming of a better life,
vanished a distant traveler
into a dark land.
Never hearing word of his again
the flashing smile of exuberant nights
became remote
and sometimes catacombs of thoughts,
or sudden collision with embarrassing past
stirs the silent tomb, unmasked,
on which I sit,
making me dream of some small plot of earth,
where lies a friend.

Passionate Search

No man has known madness save in the chain-like spell that life casts across each man's shadow. For man was born of two strange passions. The dark pulsing beast, forever pounding, pounding at the portals of the heart, which in daylight forever cries for fury and an end to rest. And then the bog-like spell of night, the gentle lover, who lulls all hope of wandering from the guileful by sweet temptations of woman's flesh. Never, never, screams the youth defiant, who seeks to cross great oceans, hear the voices of ten million men, see all the faces that the earth can bear, and know the very core of man through the channels of his many tongues.

Temptation

The end to time
which all men taste
is the dread prompter
for his puny act.
He sneaks upon life's stage one dawn,
ignores hints of the future,
performs the gawkish dance of youth
then turns prurient,
sad teens jumping and hopping
into the next niche in man's life.
The passing youth who seeks
for all that time denies,
finds the temptress,
whose maddening smile
lures him from the promise
of a glimmering future.
Some frigid wench
closes all doors to higher hopes
for the last dread run
to unnoticed exit.
The end to man's intoxicated fever
which makes his scrawny bosom swell,
spurs him to defy all Gods,
cry out for art, plead for love,
down the time worn paths
where harlots wave farewell.

Schemers

You the penny candy
of wide-eyed children,
the red, green sour ball,
disremembered taste
of some lone ranger, green hornet,
inner sanctum ago,
fearing paunched men
lurking in steamrooms,
whose sweat runs like mice
escaping pursuers.
They have pink mouths,
hungry jowls,
are never sated.

Forgetful

Withering song
escaping from the morning glow
as your soft body
wriggles into life.
O that freckled flesh
I touched last night
touched me,
led me to a chamber of forgetfulness.
I was so much you
that afterwards
we were just one,
spinning,
finally falling apart
as new as birth.

Time Lag

No longer our time
but that of lassitude,
withering a dream,
a night of passion,
until riddled with decay,
I sleep and dream
of Butterfly's lament,
rocking my cradle body
in a vision of exotic shores
that ends my travels
when I awaken.

Perspective

I am the man
whose steps of silence tread
the shore of darkness,
while many rivers flow
in currents that sing
of our million years
of loneliness and sorrow.
The harsh beast cry
stirs the root of memory
with forgotten anguish.
The river speaks,
the moment-living wake
pounces on the shore:
"One thousand years of man go by
as pebbles cast into the sea
and all his gods are born and die.
Another thousand years go by
with time's dread fingers erasing
fears of the future."

First Poem Sent – Oct. 1962

I wrote a poem
and worked on it.
With some hesitation
I bought an envelope and stamps,
addressed a famous magazine.
I brought it to the post office
and gave it to the postman.
Without a glance
he tossed it on a pile
and it fell to the floor.
What will happen to this exile
from my unprotected soul?

The Spirit of Man

To the spirit of man in the night,
who vigils of loneliness keeps,
between visions of deep inner light
and frail brothers for whom he weeps.
For sorrows that breed in the span
that truth and love do last
in the weary spirit of man
until his desire has passed.
Then in the self new born
a grandiose vision seemed
to promise that fear was outworn
and hope would soon be redeemed.

Sleepy Brooklyn

The streets of time are silent.
Across the expanse of Brooklyn
a midnight silence hangs.
The sly noises of late residents
 trying to conceal after-hours wantonness
rasp clumsily on somnolent streets.
The slumbering residential streets echo
dying footsteps of a reckless night wanderer,
 returning after his fellows have gone to bed.
The distant blare of a car horn
temporarily stirs rem addicts,
who recede into oblivion.

Lethe

We express our suffering
in the song of traveling sorrow,
as we mourn for forgetfulness
on a thousand lonely roads
that our bleeding feet
traverse to find oblivion.
Some desperate seekers
yearn a master painter,
blame the mixer for creating
the canvas of gnarled humanity,
who cruelly prevents
the fulfillment of dreams.

Trace Memory

I remember the nights
when our flesh would fall together,
exploding us higher than destruction,
her breasts tiny bombs
waiting to detonate
in my cowering hands….
But that was long ago
and I know not where she went.

Corruption

The subtle subversions
that we often miss
evade public combustion,
and spill from gushing palates,
cackling like greedy seagulls,
as they peck and fawn
around nourishment sources
poking their avid beaks,
depravedly indifferent mammals,
gorging on the body politic.

Urgent Youth

The summer nights in the city are torpid, breeding indolence in lonely youths standing on street corners in ten thousand similar poses, waiting desperately and sometimes violently for any diversion to change the tortuously dull problem that must be faced daily; what to do. Each outer borough has hordes of uncontrolled, undirected boys, roaming the streets from the end of June to early September; prurient in their ripening needs, yet denied access to blossoming girl-flesh to sate their needs. Thus vast numbers of urgent, frustrated boys plot the brief vacation days away with frequent and repetitive yearnings to obtain a girl. How often have we seen them, rowdy, self-conscious and impatient, moving noisily through Coney Island, Times Square, Greenwich Village, other lurid spots of the indifferent city, making smutty remarks to passing girls, since negative reactions are better than none at all. They are forever denied satisfaction. For most of them there are days that gleam and never come again. Days that almost burst with the current and power of youth. A mighty tide of curious confusion, senseless, empty actions and directionless endeavor, leaves them stranded in our alien land.

Familial Place

How often have I stood in this very place, beneath the frigid hangings of the ancient ghosts of my fathers. How many times, when caught in the passion of some new discovery, have I stood before the massive seat of judgment and heard my dreams consigned to fade away; untasted, unsavoured. And thought most bitter, to be set aside, deposited, left to age, moulder in the cellar of my mind, until dessicated with misuse and left to crumble my remaining hopes.

Hard Times

We have dreamed of time and hunger as we sat alone, burning in a midnight land of strangers. We have sent our flaming cry across the dark, chaotic waste engulfing us. Why can't we see a gentle face? Through burning ache and barren search we sometimes feel the bright surge of hope that lights up the long, long night. Most often we see the twisted frames of frightened men, who whimper in their sleep, and hear the late night throb of dreams that yank them awake, leaving them adrift in sweaty sheets.

Domesticity

Wanting you
not in circumspect discretion,
but letting the explosive madness show,
until your knowing, testing,
then letting me take you,
erupting an insane hunger
swallowing you,
chaining you inside me.
Secure,
a mocking laugh startles me,
stabs in midnight whispers.
I whimper awake,
your head beside me on the pillow,
little girl's face crinkly with sleep.
I shake you.
I scream your name.
I shatter you awake.
I cry: 'Do you love me?'
'Whatta you crazy?' you yell.
'I gotta go ta work in the morning.
Lemme sleep.'
You mumble: 'Dopey sonofabitch.'
Pat me.
Not knowing to caress or strangle,
I lie rigid, staring at the ceiling,
you asleep. I awake.
The alarm rings,
you stretch,
shut it off,

roll on me,
prison me beneath you,
run your tongue along my neck and under my chin.
Whisper: 'My possessive little boy.'
Your hand takes root on me.
You weld us together.
You moan an ecstatic ghost cry of tremors,
then still.
We doze.
With you melting on me,
the long night fades.

A Long Nights Burning is Our Life

We dream of time
and sit alone
 in midnight lands of hunger.
Dark, chaotic waste engulfs us,
pointing only for a moment
to start a distant hand,
groping, touching, parting.
We cannot sleep
and cry to see the strangeness fade.

Grim Chaos

In my day of earthly sorrow
I tell my spirit be serene,
soon I'll see the long tomorrow
after that the end of the dream.
Then in the blaze of freedom
I'll quench my burning thirst,
forget the earthly kingdom
in which my spirit burst.
When the world no longer measures
dreadful things will cease to be,
great pain will change to pleasures,
great joy will terrify.

Dashed Hopes

In the night,
where sorrow and the lost sit
forever in the thoughts
of day's wisdom,
murmuring of spirits
that once trod the earth
in visionary realms of phantasy
of the hungry stride of time
in the cavern of darkness,
with memory and thought
our sole companions,
we watch with famished eyes
a lovely maiden
who we most potently desire
pass and be lost
in the vast man-tide,
the shock that bursts
the frail bubble of dreams.

Abandoned Youth

Pollution plumes drift over slum streets
that smell of sabotage,
with babies peeing in the gutters,
while bands of predatory youth
steal past the sleeper's windows
in the still moments of the night.
Across the backyards
the countless eyes of night leer.
The drone of nagging wives,
husbands turning sour,
and the children screaming,
who forsee their future.
They pour from isolation,
cry for all that's missed,
curse only from despair,
then pick up the rusted pieces
of their tormented lives.
Only insomniacs see them run
in skinny-legged groups,
down filthy, barren streets,
past tenements of dank dirt
that fill the haunted dreams of youth.

Painful Search

I sat within myself one day
and saw my spirit rise,
and wave a blade of searing fire
before my sleeping eyes.
I felt my weary mind awake
and cast off fetters deep
and leave the cell my thoughts had made
with manacles of sleep.
I searched with famished eyes and ears
for signs that I was free,
but only found confusion's angst
and knew it could not be.

Final Sentence

Wishes are never horses,
but sullen malcontents
seeking an easy mount
to avoid tough decisions,
how to treat calculating murderers
who do not hold life sacred
and evoke our charitable forgiveness,
when we should execute them,
like turkeys for Thanksgiving.

Momentary Ease

At last it is the woman
who wearily whispers
in after-love exhaustion.
With her sweet, tired loins beside me,
her thoughts press close
with unhidden warmth,
drawing us together
for a brief moment,
before final separation.

Commuter

When I hear a great ship
cry its ghost-cry
in the night,
masters of the rich world,
I want to ride your waterways,
until the sun sets on harpies,
lying on Miami beaches.

Weak Society

Softly a summer wind flows
and brings forth a rapture
of sweet forgetfulness.
Murmurs from our depths of sorrow,
cry of pain caused by betrayals
for few will comfort the weak and despairing,
when oppression summons all of us
to cease from righteousness.

Night Thoughts

I sit in my dark room quietly absorbing the night. The wind rustles the undergarments of the trees, making them sway in solemn dance. Obscure voices drift through the open windows, penetrating my semi-consciousness. "But her teacher said she couldn't. I got angry and sent a letter…." "Aw. They never care what you say." "And she sent me a very nice answer, telling me how good she is in …." "In what?" I asked silently. I pushed them away, into the domain of night which holds so much of empty conversation in its tired bowels.

My upstairs neighbor, giving vent to his incompetence, repeatedly screams at his wife: "You're a dog. You're a dog." On and on, until the night becomes aware of his emptiness, his obsession. I picture him grotesquely lumbering around a fire, chanting strange monosyllables to whatever gods he feared, until daylight found him sprawled across the remnants of his fire, oblivious to everything but his primitive dreams.

I can see the school next door; empty, remote, lusterless as a tomb. Within that building, I muse, the lives of so many innocents are mutilated. The empty corridors, classrooms, desks that I visualize finally feel to me the way they must feel to the child, who gropes for help in this labyrinth of confusion that is frigid, barren and eternally damning.

Politicians

Pour forth
the tempestuous torrent
of bitter loathing
in undying combat
against fetid workers of speech,
for deceptive rhetoric
that assails the portals
of our isolated people,
targets of manipulation,
as they try to persuade us
to share their sty.

Doomed Youth

Pity the ardent youth
lost in helpless passion,
or locked in hopeless love,
while in his tortured silence
demons in cowls
wearing ravenous scowls
quite consume him.

Preferences

To some of us,
love is a pet-shop window
full of puppies,
rolling, cuffing, nipping,
but a cranky old woman
much prefers cats,
with whom she discusses Heidi.

Idi

The mad Dictator
runs on swift legs for power.
His eyes the hunger of zoo animals.
The empty bellies of children do not disturb him.
He is determined on his cruel course,
an explosion awaiting detonation.

Stasis

Far from grassy hills I wander,
amid the waste of my desire,
while much of me I squander
because I dare temptation's fire.
The pillars of my strength lie low
and in despair I wallow,
since roads I travel do not go
in the ways I should follow.
So my weaker self is flailing
as I curse my confused state,
with my feeble efforts failing
I do nothing else than wait.

Prowl

The night yowl
of the alley cat
with the earthly sorrow
of nine lives,
rends the silent air,
awakening the slumberers
from infinite reveries
in soporific dreams
of earth madness,
fettered only
by the bonds of sleep.

Summons

I call to Americans
before it is too late
to prevent our destruction.
Purposeless generations
must be reeducated
to recognize the threat
from the greedy men
behind the flight of capital,
who do not care
if we survive or perish.

Lyrics

Burnout

I've got burnout,
burnout,
it sure makes me down.
I've got burnout,
burnout,
it sure makes me down.

Couldn't find no more blues,
it sure makes me down.
Lost my denim jacket,
it sure makes me down,

I've got burnout,
burnout,
burnout's sure a down.

Ran out of uppers,
best friend went to jail,
my girl said goodbye,
but knew I wouldn't die,
knew I wouldn't die....
Don't want nothing else.

I've got burnout,
burnout gets me down.

Burnout makes me sit around
 just nodding up and down.
Nothing else to do.

Don't go out no more.
There's nowhere left to go.

I've got burnout,
burnout,
no where left to go.

Things Will Go Right, Someday

We don't have
the fun we used to,
worrying about money,
fantasies of success.
envying others
not content with what we have.

Nothing seems to go right.
Dreams are just out of sight.

Everyone's getting fatter,
nothing tastes good anymore.
All we're left with
are our fragile hopes
that someday, somehow,
things will go right.

I Don't Want

I don't want a limousine,
my picture in a magazine,
just don't want to be alone.

I want someone
whose mind's not blown.
There must be someone,
somewhere out there,
looking for an honest friend.
I don't know if I'll find her,
but my search won't ever end.

I don't want a limousine,
my picture in a magazine.
I just don't want to be alone.

Hold on Tight

Hold on tight,
the world is spinning
much too fast.
Hold on tight,
nothing's going to last.
Can't take hold,
everything I want's
just out of reach.
Can't take hold,
nothing seems to work,
so hold on tight,
nothing's going right.

Show Me

I want you by my side
a long, long time.
And if I forget
the way I feel
for a moment or more,
show me,
show me.
For I want you by my side
a long, long time.

No matter how hard I try
I can't always be right,
for I'm just a man
and that's how I am.
So when I forget
the way that I feel
for a moment or more,
show me,
show me.

It's not that I don't care,
or that I can't be true,
but sometimes I forget,
sometimes I forget
the way that I feel
for a moment or more,
so show me,
show me,
the way that you feel

www.ingramcontent.com/pod-product-compliance
Lightning Source LLC
LaVergne TN
LVHW020337200726
843507LV00012B/2394